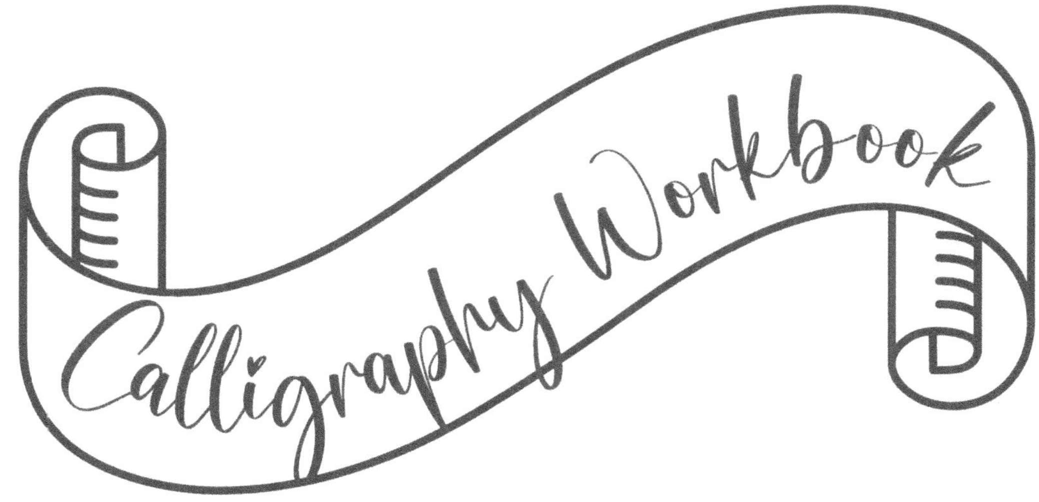

Calligraphy Workbook

By
Life Style Daily

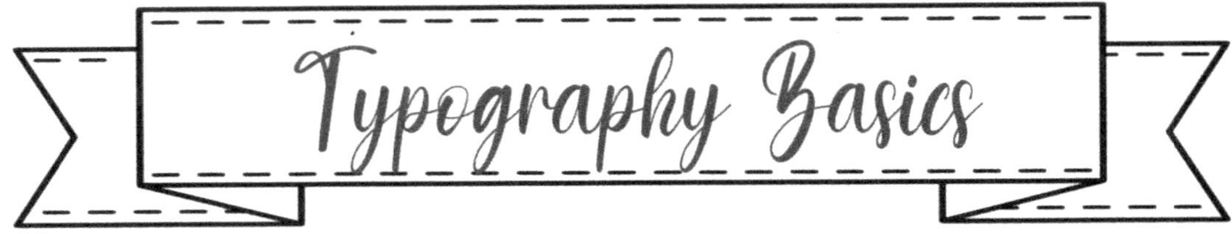

Not to make this overly simplistic, but there are some really basic things that you can do that will set you up for lettering success. In the beginning posture, pen grip and paper might seem underwhelming, but it's really giving yourself the best possible chance at mastering lettering.

Body

You might be thinking, why does this matter? Well in lettering, or calligraphy (I use the words interchangeably although some purists will say that's wrong. Luckily, they're not the boss of me) the movement of your pen or brush is all important. You need to position yourself in a way that gives your hand and arm the freest range of motion. Which means it's incredibly hard to letter and host a dance party at the same time.

Try sitting at a desk or dining room table or some place where your feet can be flat on the ground and there's a hard surface in front of you. For good lettering you'll be moving your whole arm so it's good practice to use your non-dominant hand to hold the paper in place. This will give you greater control.

Pen

When holding your pen (or marker or paint brush or whatever fancy thing you've worked out) you want a moderate grip. Something firm enough it won't slip out of your hand but loose enough to do swirls and loops and change the pressure frequently. More on that later.

The most important thing about your pen is that it must be held at an angle. Even a brush pen is still essentially a brush and if you're going to take advantage of the brush strokes you'll need to take advantage of the actual brush. If you use it just straight up and down it's impossible to tell the difference between your soft up strokes and your strong downstrokes. You'll figure it all out, I promise.

This is a new skill, don't get discouraged if you don't get it right away. I promise you didn't pick up walking on the first try, and you fell down a lot. Thank God your parents didn't take one look at your pitiful attempts and decide that walking just isn't for you. They let you get up and keep trying again. Do that here and you'll see big results in your mindset, and probably your lettering too!

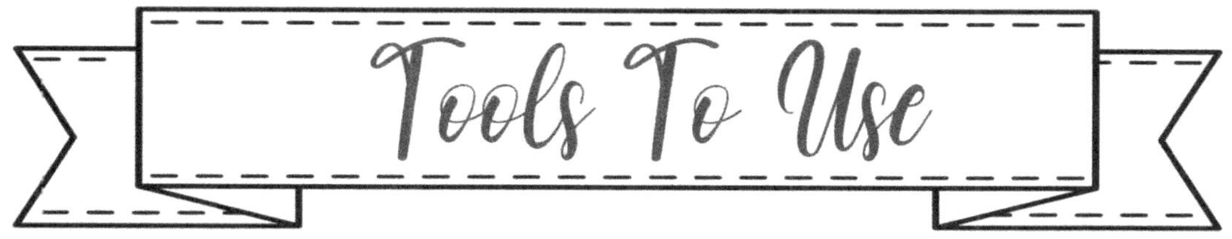

If you so choose, you can go down the crafty crazy rabbit hole and probably spend a boat load of money on supplies. If that's your jam, fantastic. For this book we're keeping it simple so we'll only be using the Fudenosuke Pen and a Brush Pen. But some typical options are:

- ★ **Pencils**
  Simple, basic, nearly everyone can find this. It's a solid option.

- ★ **Pens**
  Not sure where to start? Grab a pen. Micron pens look great, but you could get fancy with a gel or felt tip pen too and get a good monoline.

- ★ **Brush Pens**
  This is the modern version of that quill thing they used in colonial times. If you're not careful, it could become your new obsession.
  Pro tip is to avoid starting with a large and soft brush pen because it's harder to control when you're still also trying to figure out your arm movements and such.

- ★ **Watercolors**
  Yep. Real art time. They work great and you can switch up brushes at your whim for varied results. Get experimental, it's fun!

- ★ **Chalk**
  There are markers you can buy and before you know it you'll be a chalk lettering genius. It looks amazeballs and everyone loves a beautiful sandwich board on the sidewalk.

- ★ **Paper**
  We've set up this book that you can use the given space but if you want to practice on something you'll want to get some heavy grade card stock type stuff. Thin paper like printer paper is hard to use so you'll want to invest in something heavier.

- ★ **Fudensosuke Pen**
  In this book we're using a fineliner pen for the monoline script. You can order any one or pick one up at your local crafting store.

- ★ **Brush Pens**
  For our lettering together you can use a brush pen for the brush calligraphy and flourished designs.

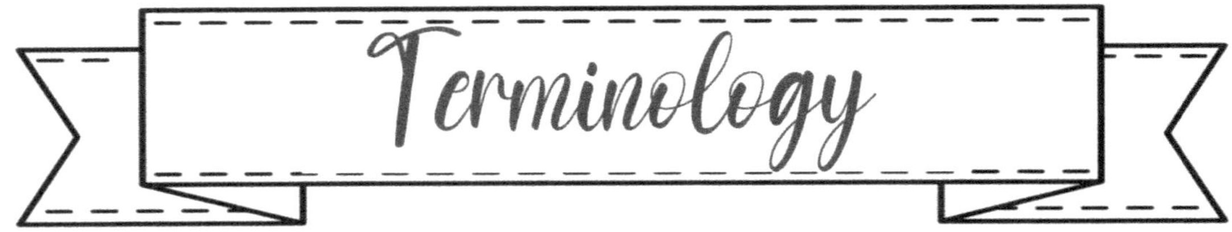

If you're going to learn to letter, we've got to get through a bit of vocabulary words first so don't start skipping pages just yet!

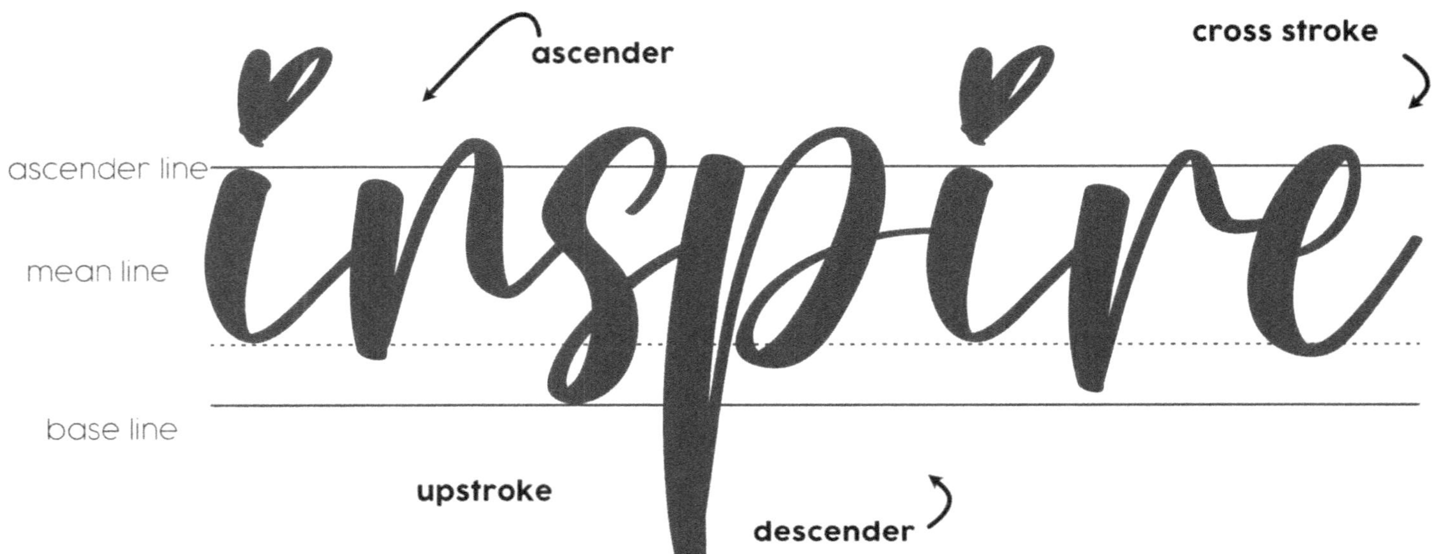

DOWNSTROKE: Any movement downward with the writing instrument. These lines are thick!

UPSTROKE: Any movement upward with the writing instrument. These lines are thin!

ASCENDER: The part of the letter that extends above the mean line (i.e. the top portion of the 't' seen here).

DESCENDER: The part of the letter that falls below the baseline (i.e. the bottom portion of letters such as 'g' and 'y').

FLOURISH: These are the added strokes and swashes used to decorate or enhance letters.

CROSSBAR: Horizontal strokes on letters such as 't,' 'f,' and uppercase 'H'.

LETTERFORM: The form or shape of a letter.

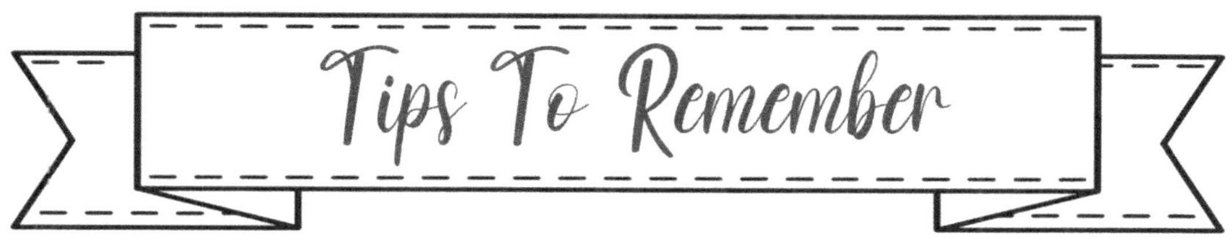

One: The most important tip is to write slowly! Think of lettering as drawing each letter, instead of just writing each letter.

TWO: Start with pencil. You can draw and erase as you fine tune your letters!

THREE: Pick up your pen in between strokes. Unlike cursive, where your pen flows on the paper through the entire word, lettering is made up of multiple strokes.

FOUR: As mentioned, in calligraphy down strokes are always thicker.

FIVE: Upstrokes are always thinner.

SIX: Practice! Master your letterforms first! Then master connecting those letters as you write full words. Once you have mastered connections, practice your composition and design!

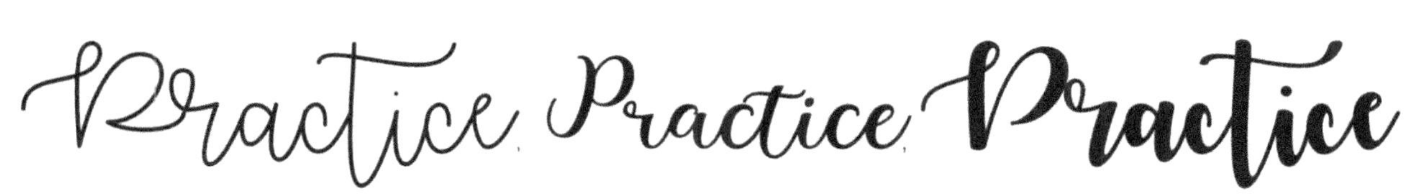

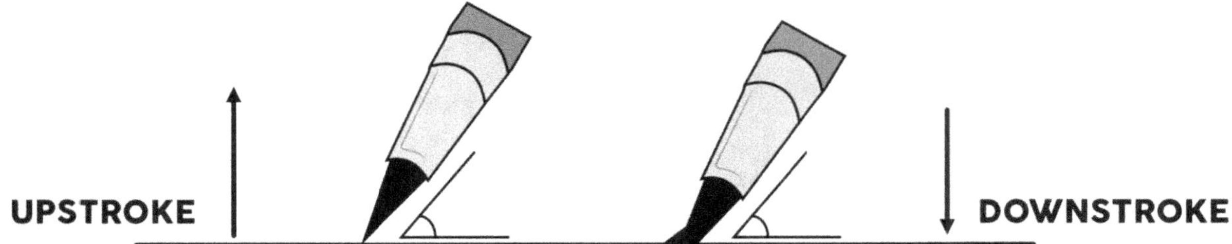

In the next section we will begin to draw our basic strokes & letterforms! Get those pencils, pens, and brush pens ready! Your lettering journey begins!

Basic Strokes

INTRODUCTION

This is also known as "fake calligraphy". I fell in love with the pretty thick strokes in my head, but in practice I love the monoline. It's faster (I think easier) and definitely channels my inner crafty Pinterest beast. You use essentially the same movements as the previous Brush Alphabet, but you keep a constant pressure as you letter. No thick down strokes here. You can bust out your pencils or regular pens here too, although the smaller tip is what I'm recommending.

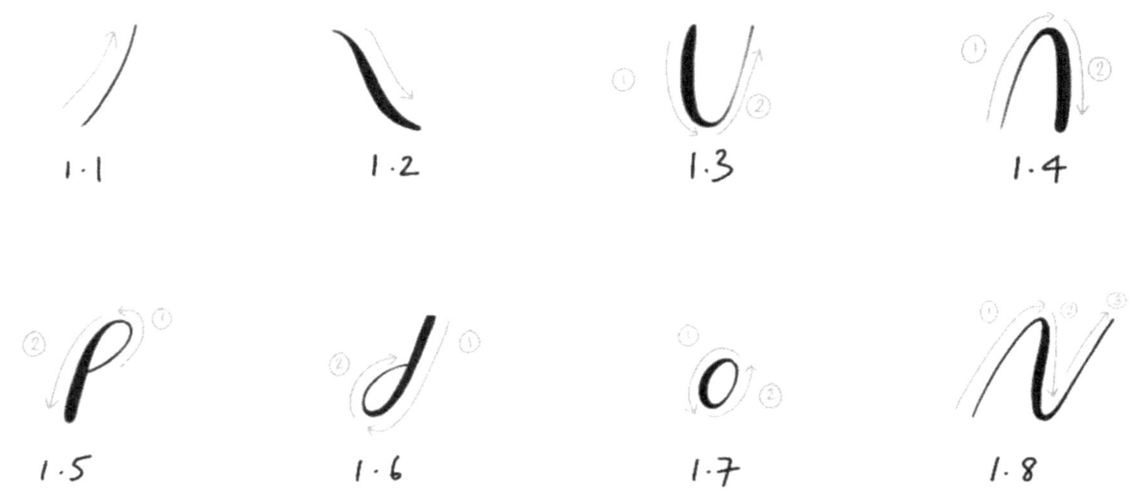

1.1   Upstrokes
1.2   Downstrokes
1.3   Underturn
1.4   Overturn
1.5   Ascending loop
1.6   Descending loop
1.7   Oval
1.8   Compound turn

Upstrokes

- starts from bottom to top/applied in an upward motion
- thin & consistent
- apply light pressure

Downstrokes

- opposite to upstrokes
- starts from top to bottom/ applied in a downward motion
  apply heavier pressure
- Start at the top, gradually moving pen down with medium pressure,
  adding more pressure as you get to the bottom
  ease off pressure at the end

Under Turn

Over Turn

- hairline upstroke, transition to thick downstroke

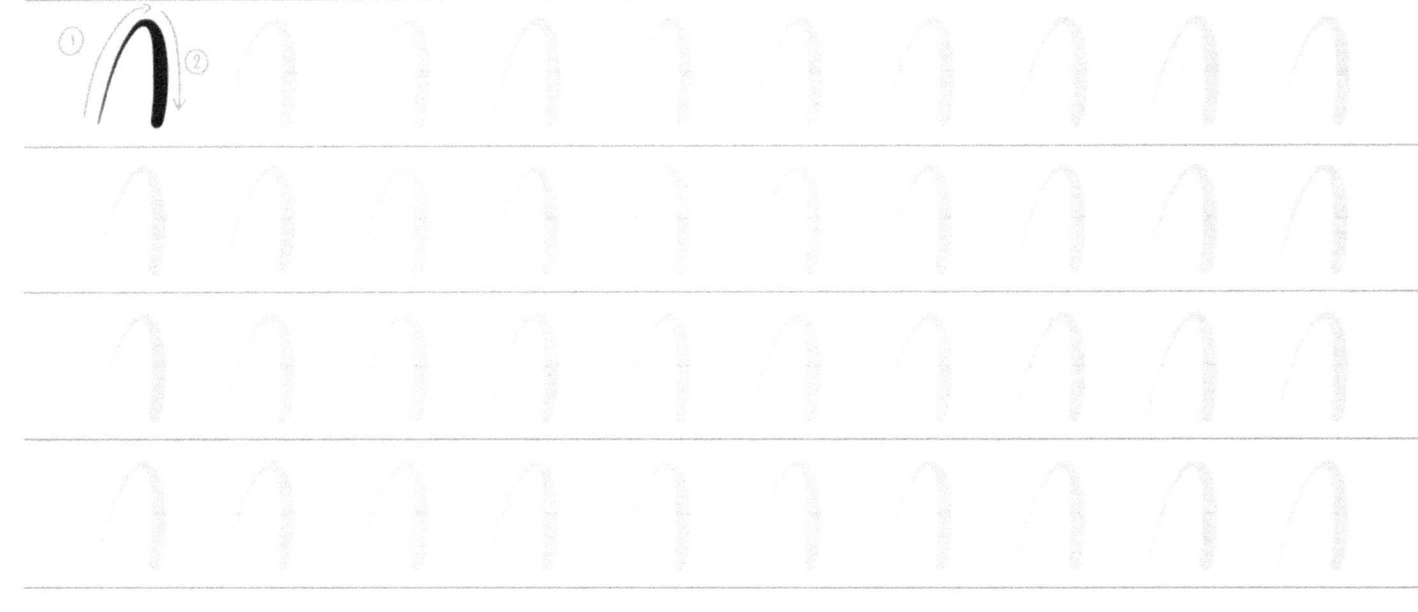

Ascending Loop

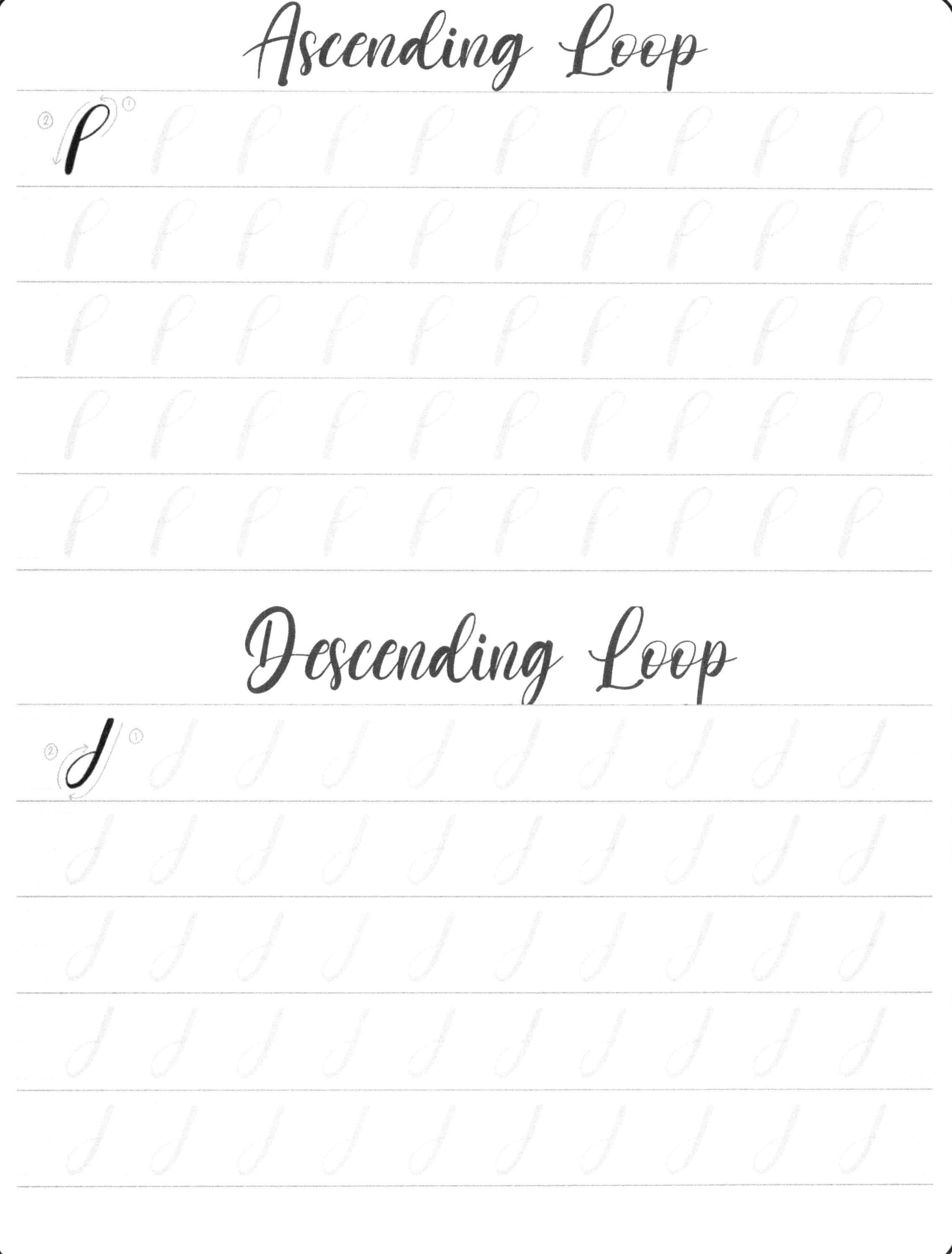

Descending Loop

Oral

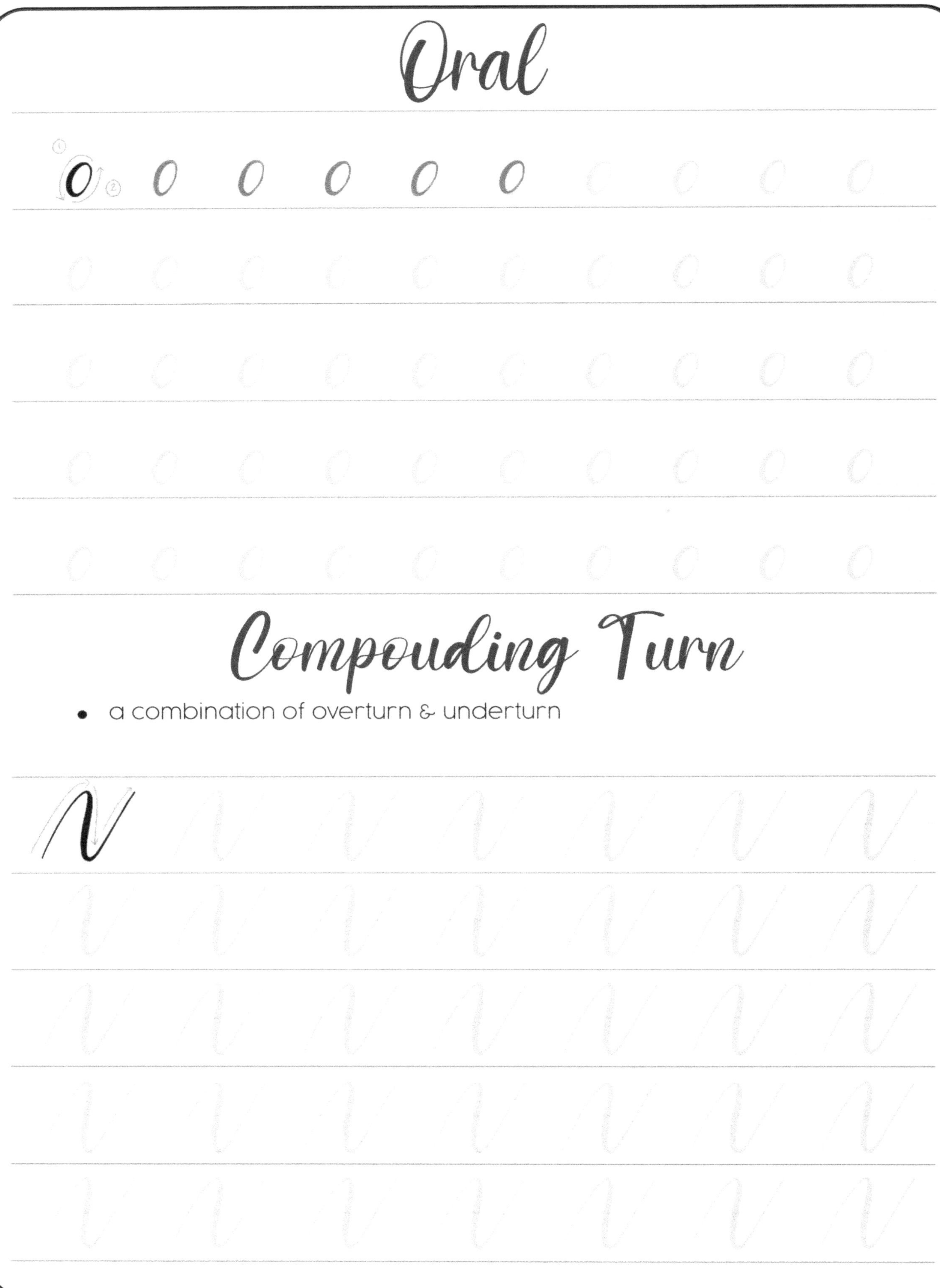

Compouding Turn

- a combination of overturn & underturn

Calligraphy Practice Vocabulary
Basic Strokes

loop

oval

arch

hook

line

dot

In every stroke, a bit of soul

Basic Calligraphy

ALPHABET - UPPER CASE LETTERS

A

B

C

D

E

F

G

Calligraphy Practice Vocabulary
Calligraphy Tools

nib

ink

grip

cap

well

pen

The nib carves emotion

Basic Calligraphy

ALPHABET - UPPER CASE LETTERS

H

I

J

K

L

M

N

Calligraphy Practice Vocabulary
Paper Types

bond

grid

vellum

laid

wove

card

Paper is the canvas of the mind

Basic Calligraphy

ALPHABET - UPPER CASE LETTERS

O

P

Q

R

S

T

U

Calligraphy Practice Vocabulary
Stroke Types

shade

hair

down

up

thin

bold

Every line is a journey

V

W

X

Y

Z

Calligraphy Practice Vocabulary
Manuscripts

book

leaf

page

text

font

size

The written word is everlasting

Basic Calligraphy

ALPHABET - LOWER CASE LETTERS

a

b

c

d

e

f

g

Calligraphy Practice Vocabulary
Art Elements

hue

tone

form

line

tint

grid

Writing is painting with words

Basic Calligraphy

ALPHABET - LOWER CASE LETTERS

h

i

j

k

l

m

n

axis
body
edge
flow
grid
peak

Balance in form,
harmony in design

Basic Calligraphy
ALPHABET - LOWER CASE LETTERS
o
p
q
r
s
t
u

Calligraphy Practice Vocabulary
Script Styles

italic

black

roman

urcial

bold

thin

Script is the dress of thought

Basic Calligraphy

ALPHABET - LOWER CASE LETTERS

v

w

x

y

z

Calligraphy Practice Vocabulary

Hand Positions

rest

grip

lean

lift

turn

drop

Each loop, a dance of the hand

Basic Calligraphy

UPPERCASE & LOWERCASE PRACTICE

A

a

wet

dry

fade

run

hue

mix

Ink flows, creativity grows

Basic Calligraphy

UPPERCASE & LOWERCASE PRACTICE

B

b

Calligraphy Practice Vocabulary
Tehnique

flow

pace

tilt

grip

pull

drag

Precision is the key to beauty

Basic Calligraphy

UPPERCASE & LOWERCASE PRACTICE

C

c

Calligraphy Practice Vocabulary

neat

fine

bold

soft

hard

clear

Quality shows in every line

Basic Calligraphy

UPPERCASE & LOWERCASE PRACTICE

D

d

Calligraphy Practice Vocabulary

Composition

form

rule

unit

part

span

spot

Creativity within constraints

Basic Calligraphy

UPPERCASE & LOWERCASE PRACTICE

E

e

Calligraphy Practice Vocabulary
Anatomy

foot

head

tail

body

neck

arm

Every stroke courts

Basic Calligraphy

UPPERCASE & LOWERCASE PRACTICE

F f

f

Calligraphy Practice Vocabulary

Spacing

kern

lead

gap

room

snug

wide

Unity in diversity of forms

Basic Calligraphy

UPPERCASE & LOWERCASE PRACTICE

G

g

slab

thin

hair

flat

long

short

Elegance lies in the flourish

Basic Calligraphy

UPPERCASE & LOWERCASE PRACTICE

H

h

Calligraphy Practice Vocabulary
History

Rome

quill

reed

ink

clay

pith

The essence of tradition in a letter

Basic Calligraphy

UPPERCASE & LOWERCASE PRACTICE

I

i

Calligraphy Practice Vocabulary

Cultural Scripts

kana kana kana kana kana

deva deva deva deva deva

arab arab arab arab arab

thai thai thai thai thai

tibet tibet tibet tibet tibet

greek greek greek greek greek

Lettering is structured imagination

Lettering is structured imagination
Lettering is structured imagination

Basic Calligraphy
UPPERCASE & LOWERCASE PRACTICE

J

j

Calligraphy Practice Vocabulary

Level

easy

hard

soft

fast

slow

fire

Skill is honed, not born

Basic Calligraphy

UPPERCASE & LOWERCASE PRACTICE

K

k

Calligraphy Practice Vocabulary

Inking Tools

jar

well

dish

pad

tray

tube

Ink is the blood of calligraphy

Basic Calligraphy

UPPERCASE & LOWERCASE PRACTICE

L

l

Calligraphy Practice Vocabulary

Practice

loop

curl

flip

twist

pull

drag

Practice makes permanent

Basic Calligraphy

UPPERCASE & LOWERCASE PRACTICE

M

m

Calligraphy Practice Vocabulary

Adjustments

trim

set

tilt

bend

turn

size

Refinement comes with repetition

Basic Calligraphy

UPPERCASE & LOWERCASE PRACTICE

n

n

Calligraphy Practice Vocabulary
Pressure

firm

soft

hard

light

even

vary

A steady hand, a steady mind

Basic Calligraphy

UPPERCASE & LOWERCASE PRACTICE

Calligraphy Practice Vocabulary

Guideline

line

mark

rule

grid

path

zone

Discipline creates freedom in form

Basic Calligraphy

P

p

Calligraphy Practice Vocabulary

Corrections

wipe

blur

trim

cut

tack

mend

Craftsmanship over shortcuts

Basic Calligraphy

UPPERCASE & LOWERCASE PRACTICE

Calligraphy Practice Vocabulary

Materials

wood

cork

felt

wool

silk

clay

Ink speaks where words fail

Basic Calligraphy

UPPERCASE & LOWERCASE PRACTICE

R

r

Calligraphy Practice Vocabulary
Holding Styles

fist

palm

claw

hook

pinch

grip

Grace is found in the stroke

Basic Calligraphy

UPPERCASE & LOWERCASE PRACTICE

Calligraphy Practice Vocabulary

Swasches

loop

tail

hook

curl

arch

wawe

The beauty of form over function

Basic Calligraphy

UPPERCASE & LOWERCASE PRACTICE

T

t

Calligraphy Practice Vocabulary

Themes

love

peace

wish

hope

calm

joy

Words become art
in skilled hands

Basic Calligraphy

UPPERCASE & LOWERCASE PRACTICE

Calligraphy Practice Vocabulary

Time

hour

day

week

month

year

era

The quill reveals the inner quill

Basic Calligraphy

UPPERCASE & LOWERCASE PRACTICE

W

w

skill

art

trade

work

task

form

Handwriting is a skill,
calligraphy is an art

Basic Calligraphy

UPPERCASE & LOWERCASE PRACTICE

X

x

Calligraphy Practice Vocabulary
Motion

drag
lift
stop
start
snap
flip

Flow is the essence of calligraphy

Basic Calligraphy

UPPERCASE & LOWERCASE PRACTICE

Y

y

Calligraphy Practice Vocabulary

Variants

tone

form

line

hue

tint

size

Subtlety defines sophistication

Basic Calligraphy

UPPERCASE & LOWERCASE PRACTICE

$\mathscr{Z}$

z

Calligraphy Practice Vocabulary

Contrast

dark

light

bold

thin

high

low

Artistry lies in the details

Connections And Words

LOWERCASE BRUSH

You're doing great lettering! Give yourself a pat on the back for making it this far and keeping going. Celebrate your wins.

Don't forget to pick up your pen after each stroke and keep going! You're already a kick butt letterer.

a b:

g r:

s w:

d o:

m i:

l a:

c h:

l l:

Calligraphy Practice Vocabulary

Care

clean

wipe

wash

soak

store

dry

The soul of calligraphy
is serenity

Connections And Words

LOWERCASE BRUSH

h i:

p r:

s t:

o m:

b o:

l i:

q u:

e x:

e n:

Calligraphy Practice Vocabulary

Types of Nibs

broad

fine

flex

quill

flat

stub

The pen is mightier than the sword

Connections And Words

LOWERCASE BRUSH

You're doing great lettering! Give yourself a pat on the back for making it this far and keeping going. Celebrate your wins.

Don't forget to pick up your pen after each stroke and keep going! You're already a kick butt letterer.

a b :

g r :

s w :

d o :

m i :

l a :

c h :

l l :

Calligraphy Practice Vocabulary
Design Elements

logo

icon

trim

bar

box

tag

Calligraphy:
where art meets text

Guideline Practice Sheets

Guideline Practice Sheets

Guideline Practice Sheets

Guideline Practice Sheets

Guideline Practice Sheets

Guideline Practice Sheets

Guideline Practice Sheets

Guideline Practice Sheets

Guideline Practice Sheets

Guideline Practice Sheets

Final Remarks

As you reached the final pages of "Calligraphy Workbook," we hoped you found yourself not merely at the end of a book, but at the beginning of a newfound mastery or deepened understanding of the art of calligraphy. This workbook was crafted to provide a comprehensive and structured approach to calligraphy, enriched with carefully chosen word sets and inspiring quotes to elevate your practice. Whether you were taking your first steps or refining your advanced techniques, we trust that this resource proved invaluable in guiding you through the multifaceted landscape of calligraphic artistry.

It wasn't just about perfecting individual letters but about grasping the rhythm, flow, and balance that transformed simple alphabets into artful compositions. The skills you acquired and honed throughout these pages are not only applicable to paper but can also be translated into various creative projects and aspects of life that value precision and beauty.

Thank you for dedicating your time and effort to work through "Calligraphy Workbook." We were honored to have been a part of your artistic journey and look forward to hearing about your future accomplishments in the field of calligraphy.

With warm regards,
The "Life Style Daily" Team